AT THE FRAYING EDGE OF HISTORY

ⓑ

DERBY STANZA POETS

AT THE FRAYING EDGE OF HISTORY

First published in paperback format by Coverstory books, 2024

ISBN 978-1-10686701-8-3

Copyright © 2024: Phil Askham, Joseph Chaplain, Isabel Footring, Simon French, Jim Friedman, Ian Gouge, Emmaline O'Dowd, Dave Smith, Roy Woolley

The right of the individual poets to be identified as the authors of their work has been asserted by them in accordance with the Copyright, Designs and Patents Act 1988.

The cover image was designed using the Adobe suite of products © Ian Gouge, 2024

All rights reserved.

No part of this publication may be reproduced, circulated, stored in a system from which it can be retrieved, or transmitted in any form without the prior permission of the publisher in writing.

www.coverstorybooks.com

Phil Askham

Fitzroy 7
Barnsley Sky 8
Watershed 9
The Door Slammed Shut 10
The Polish Ice Cream Girl at Queens Park 11
Portland Bones 12
Desert Island Proposition 13
The Tea Service 14

Joseph Chaplain

mirror 17
a picture of the future 18
The Raven and the Dove 19
There's a shark in the swimming pool, ... 20
the flea 21
Garland 23
A Clown Explodes 24

Isabel Footring

St Cuthbert's Way – a journey to the far North
   Covid haibun 27
   This New Year 28
   Prayer to St Cuthbert 29
   Lady with a Unicorn 30
   Fragment 1: 31
   Fragment 2: 32
   Fragment 3: 33
   Fragment 4: 34

Simon French

Tying the Knot 37
The Boy with UFOs in His Pocket 38
Hippodrome 39
She Has Territory 40
The Great Tombola in the Sky 41
Marine Parade 42
Angel 43
Shipwrecked 44

Jim Friedman

Bulbs	47
Fog	48
Of a heart	49
'nel mezzo'	50
Man and dog	51
In little	52
Portrait of Elizabeth I as Nature	53
The stanza of a rose	54

Ian Gouge

inside out	57
They've taken down the signs for lunch	58
Life-lessons in Meccano	59
"Describe Keswick"	60
First-term Crush	61
The Cottage Hospital	62
escape	63
Words	64

Emmaline O'Dowd

Evidence	67
At the crematorium	68
Push mower	69
A mirror	70
Journal	71
Two bulls	72
Myfanwy	73
Stacking the wood.	74

Dave Smith

Catching The Impossible	77
Who's A Pretty Boy?	78
The Triumph	80
Lady Chatterley's Trial	82
Motorcade, 1963, Ireland	83
White As A Ghost	84

Roy Woolley

Signals 87
Aspects of Summer 88
The Waiting Room 89
Tuned Mass Damper 90
Before the Healing Window 91
Kitchen 92
from The Hearing Woods 93

*

Phil Askham

Phil Askham is retired academic writer of text books, research papers and professional magazine articles. Upon retirement he joined a local writers group attempting short stories at first before settling on writing poetry as therapy.

Fitzroy

Gale force warning 9:54
Wednesday twenty-seventh
force nine westerly backing

increasing storm force ten
cyclonic wind south westerly gale
eight occasionally seven

sea state rough for at least a time
thundery rain or showers
moderate visibility.

Go west Finisterre end of the world
as far as you would ever stroll
to listen to that forecast

even though sea area changed
as I thought about Camino Way
reflecting on walking's purpose.

Never completed the pilgrimage
to explore my end of the world
just solitary journeys

in search of deeper meaning
that digs deep into my spirit
determined and inspiring

trained for physical fitness
all packed into a simple sack
thinned to absolute minimum.

This is a mental exercise
leading to transformation
touching simplicity, A to B.

Fitzroy took over the end of the world
knew what to do with the weather
before he encountered his own Finis Terre.

Barnsley Sky

Sitting on the thinly upholstered seat
of the maroon South Yorkshire commuter train,
not built with comfort in mind,
opposite benches, facing each other
our cramped knees meet.

This common ground
found,
I look up from my papers
and joke about Bill's mother
and about why the Friday Barnsley sky
is always black.

In looking up I spot his
anachronistic lamb chops
and dotted neckerchief,
the sort that might wrap possessions
on setting out to seek a fortune.

Hands.
His redundantly plump, industrial,
contrast with hers, arthritic but still delicate
in their pink fingerless mitts,
his left, her right, intertwined.

We always phone home at Wombwell
she said
to check she will be there.
And then the football floodlight pylons
pass by, signalling time to get up.

It's like this every week,
I guess
I suppose that's what makes it right,
the routine, warmth and comfort we seek
from a commonplace family life.

Watershed

(Derwent Poetry Festival)

That weekend the village filled with poets,
words fell like rain on the pavements
appearing overnight,
inundating the market square,
submerged under half rhymes
and seeping round well-constructed sonnets.
By Sunday they were everywhere.

Though hard to spot at first
with practice you got the hang;
long and short, but mostly grey,
women – older and longing for love, in
improbable but quite erotic ways,
men – some dishevelled, others smart.
Appearance alone no way to set them apart.

So I listened,
felt the rhythm
marvelled at metre and
compelling spoken verse
immersed myself in meaning
and overwhelming floods of metaphor.

They'd gone by Monday morning
absorbed into the working week,
evaporating from the flagstones
not even leaving a stain.
But like old bones revealed by a sudden flash flood
something new had been exposed
and it was never quite the same again.

The Door Slammed Shut

Doris breezed in past the back door
slamming it loudly behind her
stormed through the house on the ground floor
departing by way of the front.

Speechless he stood at the window
as Doris convulsed her way down
propelled by her turbulent anger
bent on destroying the town.

The rattle of flag pole that morning
on top of the ancient church tower
should have provided a warning
of Doris unleashing her power.

And it's not just the girls who are angry
the men folk are pissed off as well
remember Desmond two years ago
the mayhem unleashed as from hell?

I saw the size of the boulders
Desmond brought down from the hills
and the impact on Glenridding village
where repair work is going on still.

Alternate, alphabetic and gendered
the naming of storms it is said
excluding the challenging letters;
the Q, U, X, Y and Z.

Innocuous sounding perhaps but increasing
with names like Nigel and Steve
frequent with intensity unceasing
not what deniers would have us believe.

Once Doris had slammed shut the front door
and stormed across the valley
she was followed by Ewan and Ivor
Gabriel, Fleur and Holly
like hurricane Harvey in Texas
each one is sent to perplex us.

The Polish Ice Cream Girl at Queens Park

They locked me in this yellow box
and parked me by the members' stand
a summer job to earn some zlotys
before starting my degree
a chance to work on my English
and learn something of the culture
in this strange and foreign land.

And whilst I feel I'm getting the hang
of single and double scoops
of cones and tubs and 99's,
some of the other confections
a bit confusing I find:
Strawberry Split and Mini Milk,
Calippo and Rocket.

They cast me adrift in the strangest place
left 'til I end my shift, whenever that might be.
And what on earth is this game called cricket,
no one explained how it works,
and why do they stop for lunch and then tea,
at first I thought they'd finished?
Oh someone, please come and rescue me!

Portland Bones

Walk through the gate into the sacred place
follow straight and narrow grid-locked paths
by dented vases of plastic flowers.

Shuffle between slumped sarcophagi
and delicate angels with broken wings,
the monumental instability

of metamorphic marble, intrusive granite
where modest white triangles warn of death
and inscribed euphemisms disguise the truth.

Polished, utilitarian, reconstituted
the hallowed sanctity of buried bones
pervades even still these broken stones.

Hillside hagiographies, open volumes,
pages wide and petrified, some half blank,
waiting for more, waiting or forgotten.

Here everything teeters on the edge
invaded by ivy, bramble and ash,
redundant yet still sacrosanct.

And ranking within the decay and decline
stands the upright Portland oolite,
cool, unweathered reflecting daylight,

stark sentinels in stone that built cities
the continuation of a unique stock
sourced from the solitary island block.

Regimental military bearing
name, rank and number all clearly displayed,
each simple crest standing on parade.

There may be more where these come from
but we will exhaust remaining reserves
to serve the demands of conflicted worlds.

Desert Island Proposition

Come join me on my venture, a tiny island paradise
no desert this, sub-tropical, neither hot nor cold
passing seasons every year, we could both enjoy
freed from interference, apologies unmade.

A self-sufficient couple, think of the veg we'd grow
at least as many bean rows as you could ever want
and if you feel the need for meat
I'm sure there's something you can hunt.

We'd walk the empty beaches, paddle in the sea
where I would take my clothes off, teaching you to swim,
ramble through rain forests, clamber extinct volcanos,
watch the flight of hummingbirds, delight in island wildlife.

And later in the evenings, when the sun goes down
dig out the wind-up gramophone and listen to the discs.
Though I'm undecided yet, I'm certain Bach will feature
maybe in all eight perhaps, I need to think it through.

We could read The Bible, as a work of fiction
or set about the Shakespeare, performing all the plays
starting with The Tempest, a tale of island life
bags me be Prospero, you can do the sprite.

Then at least another book, you can help me choose
as well, that simple luxury; the paper and a pen
so you can watch me with those eyes
as I write my opus every night.

Then, if I may make so bold, with not a soul to interfere
if it should turn a little cold, we'll keep each other warm.
Whatever else we do each day there'll be no need for compromise.
Come my friend please think it through…what is there not to like?

The Tea Service

Stanley sweeps up the shards of Clarice Cliff,
checks out the wound on the bridge of his nose
lights up the first of sixty cigarettes
washes dry blood stains from yesterday's clothes.

Empty Bell's clutched in his squalid embrace
Oliver slumps snoring, favourite chair.
Motionless now while mid-afternoon,
charmless unconscious absorbed paranoia.

Stanley leaves early, the first of three jobs
sole breadwinner keeping up his income
single support for this comic odd couple
one stout, one thin, one out, one in.

Both charming once, amusing and kind,
like the art deco collection, very fine
now bent on a mission to self-destruct
and contrive to wipe out the best that they have.

Oliver waking starts surfing the net
infiltrates innocent neighbour's broadband
slowly thus stretching his work free days
searching online for internet porn.

Later after dark a meeting or two
at a local beauty and pick up spot
maybe with luck he'll score in the car
enterprise risky in every respect.

Stan sits at home with his TV remote
cat curled contented upon his lap
tries hard to figure why he should stay
just too afraid and alone to be free.

Reflect amid remains of broken crocks,
relationship and whisky on the rocks
I am hit in the face again and again
by the shock of violence between grown men.

JOSEPH CHAPLAIN

Joseph is a writer who lives in the Peak District.

He initially began writing poetry as part of a creative writing challenge. Since then, he has improved his craft thanks in part to the mentorship of the other poets featured in this anthology.

His style is at times absurd, surreal, intense and outlandish, drawing on an amorphous variety of subject matter for inspiration including the human condition, natural landscapes, and underground music.

His poetry has appeared in Coverstory Books' *New Contexts* anthologies, *The Rebis* and *The Crank*, and his short fiction has been featured in Crystal Peake's *Dark Folklore* anthology.

mirror

shards on the floor
grinning up at you
seven years bad luck

skin of your knuckles
broken and bleeding

it wasn't rage
shattering your reflection
nothing so extreme

sometimes our scars
come from boredom

a picture of the future

dead helicopters hang like flags
telephone lines around their necks
a thousand tons of boots
stained & scuffed with bone

twisted shells of steel & glass
the hermits make their home
scuttling from the sound of gas
pissing fire across the rubble

a mother sings to her baby
the only sustenance there is
her voice neither sweet
nor strong enough to save them

the artist makes a sculpture
from casings that cost loved ones' lives
the poet rearranges fragments
of billboard ads & picket signs

the earth resumes its trembling
distant blasts engulf the sky
another nation laid to waste
another needless sacrifice

The Raven and the Dove

His serenade is harsh, discordant
as he sings the song he's practised
for this moment
just for her.

She does not mind his melody
cutting through the morning mist
scalpel-sharp.

They were drawn together
in black and white,
an artist's sketch
before the scene is painted.
His slick coat casts a shadow
above her bridal gown.
Then, a splash of colour.

No more tune
flows from his beak.
Instead, like an obsidian blade,
he thrusts it inside her
to kiss the tender flesh
beneath her lifeless feathers.

There's a shark in the swimming pool,

said little Timmy.
But everyone just shrugged it off,
sipping their cocktails, ogling
self-consciously attained gym bodies
from beneath tinted aviators.

There's a shark in the swimming pool,
he repeated from up on the diving board.
Below him, everyone was swept up
having one-way conversations
with empty-headed people
about empty-headed things.

Why can't anybody see this?
he said, mostly to himself,
as the humdrum hum of voices drummed
a rhythm with no beat,
no beginning and no end.
A monotone drone until, at last...

Fuck me! cried someone else, *a shark!*
as panic dropped its viral load.
A symphony of screams erupted
as the first arm and leg appetiser
was hungrily devoured
and the water went from blue to red.

Save yourselves! shrieked someone
stepping-stones on people's heads
as scrambling turned to drowning,
fingers fighting for hand-holds on the side.
The shrieker dropped with a splash
and his stomach bubbled to the surface.

There's a shark in the swimming pool,
said little Timmy to himself, *huh.*
And as he watched the dorsal fin
trailing patterns of intestines,
he thought about next show-and-tell,
gutted he hadn't brought a camera.

the flea

you got yourself into a routine
waking up three hours early
to shovel sustenance down your throat
join the rat race in a sardine can
stare at a screen in a chair in a cubicle
a battery farmed human at 5% power
lunch break indulgence sags over the belt

you thought you knew what was important
plans for the weekend
upcoming holiday
what's next on TV
the football results

favourite films
favourite bands
favourite restaurants
favourite people

but all that stopped
the day the flea appeared

a giant structure blocked out the sun
long segments bent at strange angles
hairs protruding into space
all of us stared up through the clouds
and this was just its leg

conspiracy bloggers crashed the internet
street preachers felt validated or betrayed
leaving little room for in between

people were looting peacefully
nothing unnecessary
only the things they always really wanted
an old couple danced in the road
as a young couple drove
with no destination in mind

people told their friends they loved them
got drunk and sang songs in the street
cried in one another's arms
with smiles on their faces

but then
the flea jumped
as was its inclination

the sun no longer eclipsed
shone down upon the earth once more
dumbfounded the people
rejoined supermarket queues
and sleepwalked back to work

but something
fundamentally
would never be the same again

Garland

Illuminated by a switch
I see your white, pregnant body
scuttle up the beam.
The sight of you
gives me shivers.
I'm sure the feeling's mutual.

A grizzly decoration swings
in winter's draught.
Twig-thin corpses tapping
silently against the wall
beneath which we sleep
separated by a hatch.

Were they once your family
those bodies
hanging from the rafters?
The remains of your ancestors
or an orgy of enemies
slain by time?

I close the door between our worlds.
But as I do, a part of your history
falls softly to the carpet.
Something crumpled, flattened
like a mummified hand
reaching from the darkness.

A Clown Explodes

(for Alfred Jarry)

Confetti cuts of greasepaint meat
spill across the table spread.
Devilled eggs and duck foie gras,
coloured by rainbow arterial spray.

The giant daisy in his shirt
gushes blood instead of water
as that omnipresent smile
splits his face from ear to ear.

Kazoo and car horn barely hide
the howl that blasts his lungs.
Horrified guests are splattered
with his thick and slimy viscera.

A knotted line of handkerchiefs
tangles with intestines,
a juggler's coup de grâce
gives flight to eyes and testicles.

Suspenders, tendons, strips of skin
mixed up with shredded pantaloons
erupt like roman candles.
Toes rattle dice-like in oversized shoes.

Isabel Footring

Isabel started to write seriously in her early 60s. She found the confidence to develop her poetry style thanks to the encouragement she received from the Stanza poetry group. Her first poetry book *One for the Crow* was published in 2020. Since then, her poems have appeared in *First Flight*, an anthology in 2023 published by the Nottingham-based Paper Cranes poetry collective. Her short story 'The Fish' appeared in *New Contexts: 6* published by Coverstory Books in 2024.

Isabel has performed her own poetry at open mic venues in Derby and Nottingham. She co-hosts DEDA Poets, an open mic evening in her hometown, Derby, where she also promotes the work of fellow Midlands poets at the Derby Book Festival.

Her writing is inspired by the natural world, and the way legends and myths still resonate today.

St Cuthbert's Way – a journey to the far North

The poet sets off, accompanied by her good friend.

Covid haibun

I have cleaned my boots, but you, you have had a new haircut, so stylish. Your rucksack and Swedish walking poles mark you out from the dull suits and heels at Derby station.

We stomp over the bridge together, coffees in hand, to platform 6 and the York train. Settling into our seats, thankful for our Senior Railcard discounts, we pick up the threads of our conversation where we left them on the sofa, last winter.

Start of a journey, planned over the long, dark winter: white hawthorn flashing by the window, mist rising off green fields, early morning sunlight. St Cuthbert's Way, 62 miles, 5 days, beginning at Melrose on the Scottish border, finish at Lindisfarne, the Holy Island. We have bought Ron Shaw's official guide, we have planned the route and I have even lost one and a half stone so that my knees won't give me gypp on the 11th mile. And you, bless you, have booked all the rooms. St Boswell's to Harestones, Hethpool to Wooler, Fenwick to Holy Island. Over moors and drystone walls, through fell and forest, wind tangling our hair, sunburned and footsore, we walk intrepid onwards, sharing stories and secrets until at last we follow the path down to the shining grey sea. Marching across the causeway to Holy Island, sand and mud sucking at our boots, sunburned and a bit stinky, we celebrate with a foaming pint of McEwan's Export …

THIS IS A PLATFORM ANNOUNCEMENT. THE 07.50 EAST MIDLANDS TRAIN TO YORK DEPARTING FROM PLATFORM 6 HAS BEEN CANCELLED DUE TO THE PANDEMIC. WE ASK ALL PASSENGERS TO LEAVE THE TRAIN IMMEDIATELY.

Oh bitter, bitter disappointment, oh howl and gnash teeth with rage, stuck at home now, confined to house, so bored.

St Cuthbert says:
Eiderducks wait out the storm.
There's always next year, pet.

The poet starts again.

This New Year

UK has warmest New Year on record as temperatures top 15 degrees.

Longing for the Christmas lights to come down,
The proper colour of the New Year is darkness.

Sparkling the pavements with frost, freezing the night air,
The proper touch of the New Year is cold.

Thin and clear in the night sky,
The proper light of the New Year is moon.

So welcome this darkness, this cold, this moon.
I step out of my house, breathe and make three wishes.

On the Way at last, they visit St Cuthbert's cave, where the poet prays to see a slow worm.

Prayer to St Cuthbert

St Cuthbert, this I ask of thee
That I the legless worm might see.

Alreet pet.

To come upon it all alone
As it lies basking on a stone.

Alreet pet.

Although 'tis neither worm nor snake,
I ask it, Cuthbert, for thy sake.

Alreet pet.

Its skin is smooth and golden-grey.
Grant me the sight of it today.

AH SAID, ALREET PET.

Emerging from the forest, they see a hare on the path.

Lady with a Unicorn

this thread, see? nettlecloth, wool, pull this thread and it'll all start to unravel - **mother the woods are unravelling the woods are unravelling mother** - arching border of briars and outlandish strawberries all seeded into the weave of leaves, woodpecker, dunnock, cuckoo, woven on a background of faded blue – **mother the woods are unravelling** - the hare on the path, the deer in the glade, the blades of grass, the grass - **the woods are unravelling mother** - and in the leaf litter beneath the feet of the Lady are all the Fantastical Beasts - **the woods are unravelling mother** - glow worms and dingy moths - the woods are unravelling - gall wasps, woodlice and green iridescent flies - **the woods are un** - staghorn beetle and centipede, cockchaffer and unicorn - **the woods are** - woven, unwoven, warp and weft, what's left - **the woods** - fade fading - **the woods**

mother?

The poet uncovers four Anglo-Saxon fragments concerning the life of St Cuthbert.

Fragment 1:

The Abbess Hilda's temptation
(The Abbey, Whitby)

He has no home or wife.
A woollen robe his body's only house.
All summer he itches and sweats.
All winter he shivers with cold.
He shares his house with louse and flea
But will not share with me.
Yet when he dies
And death sees his body rise,
He will be clothed
In what I wove –
A linen robe without a seam,
And woven into every row,
My love for him.
I thought about his body
All my life.

Fragment 2:

The Venerable Bede's riddle
(The Scriptorium, Jarrow)

His mother gave him one life.
He lost it in Christ.
After he died
I gave him two more.

Fragment 3:

King Oswyi's conundrum
(The Castle, Bambrough)

He owns a gold and garnet cross
The size and breadth of my right hand
Yet lives in poverty.

He has no hair
Yet combs the hair he doesn't have
With comb of ivory.

Is sought by kings
To talk of peace and heal the land
Yet shuns their company.

He shuns their company
Yet builds his island cell offshore
Where they must see.

Fragment 4:

The seals' invitation
(The Heugh, Lindisfarne)

They say that on midsummer's night,
the veil between the worlds is drawn aside
and there are some who can pass over that threshold.

Perhaps he's one of them.

Not that it's ever been a problem for us.
We pass between the two worlds all the time,
rolling down to the dark water below
trailing silver bubbles.
Then rising from the fishy deeps
we break the shining surface,
to snort and huff our whiskers in the still air.

We call to him, all alone on his little island.

'Put on your claws and whiskers.
Put on your seal skin
and come with us.'

'It is midsummer's night,
the air so soft, the sea so quiet,
the tide running in the darkness.
Come with us.'

'Come with us.'

We sing to him all night
and we know he hears us
because he sings back to us
in his mournful human voice.

But he doesn't come.

'Not yet', he says.

Not yet.

SIMON FRENCH

Simon French has had two poetry collections published –
Joyriding Down Utopia Avenue (Coverstory Books 2021) and *The Deadwing Generation* (Coverstory Books 2022). His poetry has appeared in many magazines and been placed in competitions. He lives in Derby, England and works full-time helping people secure social housing.

Tying the Knot

The marquee holds its breath,

striped raspberry and cream,
it trembles like a blancmange on the lawn

as a wedding rides high and white
through the gooey afternoon.

Bridesmaids are budding,
giggled pink and skipping along under lilac.

Men in baking suits and wraparound shades
storm down the ale, bellow the chummy voice

while women pose deluxe hairdos, deftly hatted,
sip over gossip, nibble at *northern* relatives.

Hopes are launched like a bouquet
and tomorrow the marquee will exhale,

neatly fold away. Creases gaining a hold.

The Boy with UFOs in His Pocket

listens to the friction of wheat
in a field of wind.
He sits in a crop-circle. Sundown.
Suffolk
assaulting his nose with distant silage,
his wrists and forearms
covered in Nazca lines of self-harm.

They'd not believed what he'd seen

In space no-one can hear you count money

May the tabloids be with you

Lunatic go home

Near the tumbledown barn
he stares at sky,
thinks had he lived
centuries ago
he could have seen God or an angel instead

then his name would have blown across the plains
like a warm wind rustling corn.

Hippodrome

An unexploded actress
was found during renovations of the abandoned city theatre.
It is believed she had been there since at least the 2nd World War.

She was discovered
under the stage by workmen digging.
A labourer stated that she was a ticking Shakespeare

who could have gone off
at any time and they had no choice
but to evacuate and seal off the offending premises.

A Council spokesman
said that due to concerns for public safety
the building will now need to be thoroughly demolished.

The theatre's new owner
remarked on it being a shame
for the local community to lose a piece of heritage like this

especially as he'd had plans
to restore it to its former glory
and bestow upon the people of the city a theatre to be proud of.

He added that experts
had now conducted a controlled explosion
to make the actress safe and she would be laid to rest

in the foundations
of the luxury apartments
he will now be building on the site. He hoped the new occupants

would enjoy her haunting monologue
twice nightly with a Saturday matinee performance.
'It will be quite a selling point' he commented, as his Mercedes
    pulled away.

She Has Territory

Sets out on bunion feet, early morning
in search of dead leaves rioting,
exhausted streetlights,

the fungal spread of graffiti,
unruly gems from smashed bottle.
Daily, demands the Authority

sweep, erase, light and re-sanitise.
Sometimes she reports
a fallen street nameplate

that's taken a kicking by yobs
or just from time itself.
Insists the name is nailed in place.

The Great Tombola in the Sky

You've nailed your heart to the long shift,
OD'd on coffee, overran a toilet break by seconds

& you're sick of those PowerPoint suits,
their filthy projections, recycled smiles

& the office anvil on your minion shoulders
for a pittance come grateful.

So you ask yourself
what kind of life this this? Your rent is loud -

your stomach forever attention-seeking.
You're reduced

to a Lotto longshot. Love the look
of being behind electric gates in the lush country.

Convinced you wouldn't change
& after all, you'll have clocks on your side

to tug out your own novel
or plan a workers' revolution

that gets cancelled due to bad weather
or worse still, good weather.

Marine Parade

This is where I stood
as the retired wilted in & out of B & Bs
& language students chased gulls.

All the while I was patient
as crafty gardens swelled into full bloom
despite the hosepipe ban

& along the esplanade
tin cans
were having the hollow percussion

kicked out of them by bare-chested boys.
The realisation
he wasn't going to show. It all feels

like a heritage attraction. I've become
a re-enactment of myself with no gift shop
selling mugs flaunting his face,

a spray of musk
to have him on my skin. I'm here
sticking pins into ghosts

who have no business
among the lovers
that scamper from keen & thrilling waves.

Angel

You fare-dodge a tram
to her apartment, jump out
by the skate park
& look up at her balcony
where she'd hang seeds for the birds.
Walk around the corner
to the churchyard. You don't
want to be recognised
so up goes your hood & you hope
you're not too late. Can pitch
your supermarket flowers
to the thermals
of a small sky over open grave.
May they crash-land on her coffin
& never stop dreaming of bees
or the wild meadow
where you & your brother
used to hang out to smoke & roll girls
who'd never tasted river water.
You text prayers to the outreach saints
& a man called Skudz.
Your stomach hollow as a promise.
You need to eat & hear her sing.
Her perfume
clings to the clothes
you never wash & you overhear
a man in pitch-black suit & shades
say it was murder. He'll break
the bastard's neck
if he gets hold of him.
You need to leave. Go home.
Check the kitchen for bread.
Missing knives.

Shipwrecked

and like turtles plodding up the beach.
Everywhere you look – sombreros, cloches,
stetsons, trilbies. Gasping.
Drying in the sun.

Then the realisation;
marooned – *I'm a panama, get me out of here!*
but not any day soon. This island is heartless
and forgot its name long ago.

It's life or death. Survival of the stylish.
Feathered predators in snazzy colours circle,
consider a fez, a boater. Already the bowlers
are planning their strategy, an incursion

into dense jungle, to look for dead wood
and with broken shells carve a primitive hat stand.
Flat caps consider scaling the rock face,
lighting a beacon

but haven't the head for heights.
Deerstalkers attempt command. This enflames
the beanies who form an uneasy coalition
with fedoras. A lone bonnet is brutally murdered.

For the want of scalp
the hattery begins its collapse;
upturned on the sand, staring at a blistered sky
they wait for rescue. Hallucinate

streets brimming with exposed heads.
The thrill of being left on trains,
in cafes or hatnapped by wind. Being mortarboards
pitched in celebration.

JIM FRIEDMAN

Jim Friedman lives in Beeston, Nottinghamshire and took up writing again when he retired. He has had poems published in magazines, anthologies and placed in competitions.
In 2022 Coverstory Books published a first collection of his poems *Standing Alone, Leaning Against*, alongside those of Dave Smith. In 2024, his second collection *A Picture's Worth* was published (Coverstory Books).

Bulbs

As the earth shrugs beneath them,

film crews go up to a high place, and look
at now, what's happening right now;
and we can glimpse and blink it when it gets
too much to see people with so little

who have to live this now for years to come.

No errata slip for this, no extra page
tipped in at the eleventh hour,
rewriting the twelfth we are witnessing
impotently on our TV screens,

seemingly repeated for the -nth time.

A young man holds on tightly to a child,
while both stare at the camera's voyeur
doing his necessary, awful job
of recording shameful consequences,

making himself just watch behind his lens.

The young man carries goldfish, plastic bag
for bowl – temporary ark; kitchen pots,
a kitten shouldered, blankets, rolls
of bedding backpacked on a road towards

a place where they are dropping fewer bombs.

Coaches emptying their refugees
at winter's terminus. Despite his state,
the young man makes room for another life,
that kitten barely clinging on, as he is,

while the earth shrugs beneath them.

Fog

A fog is floating in,
as though out here thickens with ghosts.
Nestling in tissue paper
views are absences packed away
like muffled heirlooms.

All of us walking home
look sketches of ourselves, figures
minus arms, heads, legs
there just now then half-rubbed out
under a chalky cloud.

Muslined with the damp,
we could be lost Egyptians, mummies
from Fifties' horror films,
comical night-revenants
trailing bandages of fog.

We seem dissolvable
as sugar scattered into tea.
We're East-end kings and queens
sequinned with droplets, wearing them
like evaporating pearls.

Of a heart

They lean against a wall, waiting
for their Lazarus to meet them.
And here she is, an IV-drip in tow
and doctors, too. The first sight they have had –
each other's painful fairy-tale come true
out of the nightmares they endured.

What might it be like to hear their child's heart
beating in the body of a stranger –
an engine coupled to another train,
arriving at the platform where they stand,
distraught train-spotters looking for
some vestige of the child they knew?

They listen at the chest-wall like neighbours
next-door with a stethoscope, eaves-dropping
on the sound of resurrected life,
once overheard as breathing in a cot,
now so near yet distant as a loco
passing by them at the edge of night.

That rhythm on the rails across the ties,
the sleepers sounding their 'I am, I am...',
just like this heartbeat going somewhere else.
Crumb-comfort for the dark wood, parents hug
the frail recipient and tightly hold
their overwhelming heart-to-heart.

And when the whelm lets go, their afterlife –
the mantra of a name, almost a prayer,
quietly spoken, who knows when or why,
perhaps a summoning of love still there,
feeling the lost dimensions of a heart,
no longer just a metaphor to them.

'nel mezzo'

as though the poem takes a driving test
down a one-way street
word-capers on the camber
out in the middle of the page
no kerbs to park against

bony in a little black dress
it hangs there like a spine
of ribs and vertebrae
a path of mid-stream stepping-bones
laddering its way to page-break,

centred is a liberty
a place where certain rulings don't apply
as if a Samson pushes out the margins
tumbling them like pillars
while editors of magazines say 'Don't'

take your line for a walk with Klee
discard corsets and cummerbunds
expansively allow an elongating thought
to play caterpillar on a leaf
nibbl

e ges

ff

of

t

fillet your sonnets to a fishbone leaf
lines appearing like they're something else
behaving as the sonnets that they are
trimly espaliered
centre-page

like bees let your eyes dip and dive
to feed among the blossom there
the sherbet of its pollen gifted to your tongue
the poem's Pentecost
ventriloquising you

Man and dog

(based on a print by Angela Harding)

A nightwalker stares
at an unpolluted sky,
the clean light of stars.
His dog looks back, questioning
the man's upturned head, held still

as though he's sniffing
the night. He seems diminished
in the moonlit field,
beneath a million eyes
apparently staring down.

It's just emptiness –
awesome and indifferent –
a graveyard of lights
but love seems a puny thing
in the moon's enormous room.

So late it's early.
A walk before bed. Broken
sleep. A restless mind.
A thin moment caught between
window-sill and parapet.

The dog leads them home,
to what he knows there, to find
that togetherness
briefly halted while the man
gazed out from his life at stars.

On the blue ceiling
of a winter night, a moon
of cold amazement
behind them, they walk on, both
unable not to look back.

In little[1]

Carnation is the term
limners used for faces –
those pinkish fingernail
spaces where sitters bloom
from vases of their clothes.

How slight identity
appears in miniature.
Faces just squiggles, lines –
eyebrows, lips and nostrils –
like tiny incipits

of a self's character,
the little tunes that played
repeatedly in them,
their features like a score
of hummable music.

Their garments amplify
the sounds of who they were,
while poses finesse them
further. And names enlarge
them with their histories.

Except for those Anons
whose features are their will
and only testament,
a fingerprint-sized fame.
One smudge and they'd be lost.

---

[1] An Elizabethan term for painting in miniature.

Portrait of Elizabeth I as Nature
(attrib. Nicholas Hilliard, 1547-1619) at Hardwick Hall

Way off, along the gallery's
sisal-matted, undulating street,
past the tapestries
and other portraits, there she waits.
Level with her pearl-trimmed feet,
an old electric lamp illuminates

her portrait in its gilded frame,
as if short-sighted History has tried
to read the name
just underneath her jewelled shoes,
Elizabeth. It hangs beside
a window, in the shadows.

Dressed as Nature, doll-like, stiff,
her ruff's great scoop of wired lace
pours her out as if
she wore a shop of precious stones
like coloured sweets. Upon her dress
are salamanders, snakes and swans,

behemoths and irises. Plenitude
in person, *giving* is her noun
and verb, all good
outflowing through the land of milk
and honey painted on her gown;
life teeming in its folds of silk.

It's less a likeness more a masque
of power, meant to dazzle us
with lace and damask
opulence. It served a need,
intricate and orderly as
a head of dandelion seed.

The stanza of a rose

There's a tall rose
produces cabbagey,
deep red blooms on a brick wall close
to a door not in use.
And each year, remarkably,
it comes back. Rarely watered, seldom fed
stalwart, always profuse
though taken for granted,

quietly it puts on
a brightly blowsy show
of eye-cornering crimson,
heavily-scented close up.
For something fated to give so
much pleasure yet receive so little care,
its running-over cup,
surprisingly, is still there.

Such abundance,
showing itself in stem,
root, thorn and rose. A diligence
working hard to effect
each year's imperative in them,
accomplishing the process that is bloom –
a passion to perfect
richness in a little room.

Ian Gouge

Ian Gouge has been writing for many years with over thirty books to his name, mainly novels, short stories, and collections of poetry.

In June 2023 he performed his poetic monologue *Crash* at the Ripon Theatre Festival, and at 'WordFest' in Market Rasen in 2024.

A sometime Indie Publisher, he also mentors at public writers' retreats.

inside out

outside / a crow caws / grumpy and insistent / raspingly superior

> inside / waking early / I envy / its routine
> stitched into / the fabric of who / he is

outside / the sun rises / later by a minute / than yesterday

> inside / five o-clock / edges toward winter / and a timepiece
> grumbles / in concert with / the crow outside

They've taken down the signs for lunch

'Remember that Lobster Bisque in Bruges?
My steak that melted on the tongue?'
- and the handwritten receipt we kept, now lost,
as if that could ever be enough.

Ghosts on a naked blackboard.
Traces of Chef's specials once chalked in a florid script,
the enigma of ingredients
a code no longer on the menu to be broken.

Lured by amuse-bouches, we toyed with morsels
mistaking them for sustenance,
spices dancing more in the imagination than on the tongue
a sprinkle of salt an inadequate stand-in.

Our options were infinite a lifetime ago
a mouth-watering cascade of things to try
until past their sell-by & one by one they vanished
rubbed out by an unseen hand.

Life-lessons in Meccano[2]

If they gifted you a silver spanner
as a birthright -
> one end open   right-angled
> designed for awkward spaces
> gaps too small for keen fingers
- that would help.

In plastic compartments
baseplates and connectors
> two-   four-   eight-holed
> triangles in snazzy yellow
> and wheels and bolts and nuts
> and those oh-so-silver washers.

I remember a tall crane
construction booklet-led
inserting batteries   and watching
the hook rise and fall
until the string tangled and broke.

We fabricate our lives like Meccano
missing the invisible transition
> from toy   to something else
> from where taking apart and starting again
> shifts from the anticipation of change
> to where doing so
> > is suddenly impossible.

---

[2] "Meccano is a brand of model construction system created in 1898 by Frank Hornby in Liverpool, England. The system consists of reusable metal strips, plates, angle girders, wheels, axles and gears, and plastic parts that are connected using nuts and bolts. It enables the building of working models and mechanical devices." (Wikipedia)

"Describe Keswick[3]"

"Brooding.

Not Keswick itself of course
though in the razor-edged jags on garden-wall top-stones
there is an element of threat.

And slate grey everywhere
softened only marginally by white render
its brightness a partial concession
to something just out of reach.

And when they come
flocking by the coach-load to the B&Bs
are they too seeking the unobtainable
amidst the grey and white?"

"But 'brooding'?"

"When the low cloud swings in from the west
to envelop the tops of Blencathra in an undeniable embrace
it leaves a cotton-wool of grey and white
and the vaguest memory of what was once there
the only residual sharpness
found in razor-edged jags on garden-wall top-stones."

---

[3] Keswick is a market town in northwest England's Lake District National Park, surrounded by mountains such as Skiddaw and Blencathra.

First-term Crush

Framed by toughened glass
you in silhouette above me on the stairs,
the apex of that charmless building
with its antiseptic corridors and cookie-cutter rooms
scarred with scuffs and memories.

What were you reading while you waited?
How long had you been standing there?

I recall a thick orange-spined Penguin.
Dickens perhaps. Or Bronte. Or *Middlemarch*.
I want to remember you cradling romance -
though if you carried such ambition to my room
I was too green and lily-livered to see it.

Did I know the book and now forget?
Or did I never know?

I remember red hair; your height, tall for a girl;
a physique some might have said was statuesque.
My Echo has you studying Medicine at Boldrewood
and I regret, even now, how I never
became an object for your dissection.

What would you have found in my heart, I wonder -
and what would I?

The Cottage Hospital

after "The Cottage Hospital", by John Betjeman

Beyond municipal green, a maudlin wall
splits boisterous park from red-brick castle-tall

muddling town. Here under viridian trees
Sunday-roasting families still hope for breeze

as small uncorked children gallivant and try
to mimic the zig-zag of a mazy fly

as blindly it falls prey to a spider's weave.
No slow calypso mourning song sung to grieve

for such insignificance, no rescue call
made to squat and timid cottage hospital

where unanswered phones echo the parquet'd oak
while patients bereft of navigation soak

in sweat behind antiseptic pastel screens.
Matron knows that my fate too will go unseen,

faint rasping groans of the cemetery-bound
inconsequential. She dreams herself unwound,

there beneath full fruit trees as wasps and aphids
fly-on, serenaded by the life-filled kids.

escape

when the money ran out
sometimes he would sell a toy for cash
a Hornby Pacific loco - with steam! -
traded for half-a-dozen sausages
a tin of carrots
some Cadbury's Smash

it was an odd exchange
as if they had landed in a foreign world
with a different currency
where joy and innocence had been devalued
their shares lasting no more than a week

he was a refugee of sorts
banished from his native shores
forced to acquiesce to new rules
imposed by those who should have known better

and if there was a bunker
in which he could settle
undisturbed

he did so
locking the doors to his mind

inventing new worlds to live in

Words

draw you in, collapsing spaces as
they fracture time, twist nothingness into walls,
then make walls melt. You believe in that power
and what they might whisper, inspire, or unlock.

Emmaline O'Dowd

Emmaline O'Dowd lives in Derby, and is a long-time member of Derby City Poets, which she currently chairs, and more recently, of Derby Stanza. Her work has appeared in a range of magazines, such as *Orbis*, *Acumen*, *Popshot* and *New Contexts*.

Evidence

Two certificates. Twenty-five years' service. Thirty years' service.
>*We wish you a long and happy retirement.*

Address book,
>a few pages at a time. Mostly blank.

I phoned the few numbers. People I didn't know.
>*Such a nice man. Oh he did make us laugh.* This wasn't the you
of our edged encounters.
>*Sorry to hear of his passing.*

Kind words, but none of them came to the funeral.
>Too old, too ill, too far away.

Burned with respect, with honour, brother,
>but now those meagre records are grey-white ash

as though I'd burned you twice.
>And so much left that won't burn.

Then, high above the smoke,
>two wide skeins

full of north-to south intent,
>gold-edged in the last of the sun.

And I know it's alright.

At the crematorium

While the coffin waits for the fire,
        and the celebrant says a little too much,

I watch the simple round pool
        beyond the chapel window.

Brief rain makes the surface a circle-chase.
        The wind smocks and pleats it,

turns its design in a slow spin
        then pulls out its thread,

leaves the water as smooth
        as if nothing had ever touched it.

Push mower

Memory's tied my father's wedding-gift tag to it —
*Look after it and it'll still be going strong
in thirty years. I won't be there to see it though.*
And he's not. And it's a different marriage.
As much as anything, it's the sound I want to keep —
the gentle clattering churr, the rhythm
something like the sea, swishing in, shushing back,
on pebbly Brighton beach of childhood holidays.
I expect more rust, less paint, but not to find
one tyre perished and fallen off.
It lurches, chews, jams solid. No farewell push,
painful truth already accepted, I drag it away,
fetch out instead the new Turftrimmer Mark 2,
brace myself for the obliterating roar.

A mirror

the frame's gold flowers and cherubs undamaged,
glass intact,
left leaning
among hedgerow plants
on the slope beside the path,
emptied of the gazes it used to return.

They're kind here, keep her fed and watered,
clean and neat,
hair nicely styled.
Some visits, I think of the mirror,
how it was reflecting
just a chain-link fence, a blank sky.

Journal

Like a Japanese paper house — sliding doors, movable walls,
minimal furnishings, maximum adaptability —
one room for bolt-hole, playroom, lab, lake of tears.

Snoopers might think they see it all
through those semi-transparent screens.
But I'm not alone here. Where am I

among the imposters, the costume dramas?
The views in this journal
are not necessarily of the editor.

Two bulls

1.
This is his field, his harem,
his entitlement
to gore, crush, trample
in their defence.
He wears an archaic presence
that tells you
why bulls were worshipped, why
there's one up there in the Zodiac,
changed into nine stars.

You go round another way.

2.
Seen from a slow-moving train,
an immaculate
toffee-brown herd
and a woman
whose forehead and raised palms
rest on a wall of hide,
with the clean cows, twenty or thirty,
drawn close around her
and their lord.

We gather speed, leave Eden behind.

Myfanwy

(Dedicated without permission to Mal Buck, with apologies for the liberties taken with him. His performance can be found on Youtube.)

In the big paunch taut with fluid
the amber tide
finds something small and sentimental,
plumps it up
till it bursts into his excellent underused tenor.

"Paham mae dicter O Myfanwy...."

The whole club stops —
no pint is pulled nor crisp-packet rustled,
and all the usual currency silenced.

One by one, the male-voice choir
who just happen to be visiting,
begin to halo him with whispered harmonies,
until she hovers there, the feminine ideal,
rose-cheeked, white-handed.

The moist-eyed men
mourn for the one that got away,
or think, 'Thank God I've still got her',
and while the song lasts,
are better husbands.

Then it's cheers, pot-thumping, hand-shaking —
"I didn't know you had it in you, boyo!"
If he knew, he'd forgotten.
And no-one sees Myfanwy leaving.

Stacking the wood.

The trees were just outside our boundary,
but we felt free to borrow them.
They lopped the copper beeches —
now their handless wrists ache against new sky.
They felled the queenly birches,
and a major branch dropped on our ground.
In apology, they let us keep it.
Now you chop it into logs and wedges.

I start to stack them. A task that absorbs sadness,
each piece to be chosen for a shape
to sit firm on the layer below. I soon learn
to keep back shallow splint-like strips
to tilt the bigger ones
to the stability of a slight inward lean.

Every one's an individual worth a painting —
bright orange of still-sappy heart-wood;
the rind's black, grey and silver; yellow lichen;
some still wound with ivy.

In winter, when they've dried enough,
we'll start to unbuild the stack, feed our fires
with masterworks of bark and grain.

DAVE SMITH

Dave Smith began writing poetry seriously when he retired as an English teacher. His work has appeared in a variety of publications and he has been successful in several competitions.

In 2022, his debut collection *Standing Alone, Leaning Against* — co-authored with Jim Friedman — was published by Coverstory Books.

Catching The Impossible

It's never easy to catch an invisible baby giraffe
but your plan was a good one. "Let's put out
some food that it likes so it will smell it.
An apple should do the trick," you said, standing
on tiptoe to reach the reddest apple in the bowl.

On the second attempt you heard hooves drumming like rain.
On the third, munching, like footsteps crunching on shingle.
Each time you dashed off after setting the trap,
I thought you'd stop, turn, see me slip
the apple into my pocket but you never did.

Who's A Pretty Boy?

She hadn't expected it would take so long.
All the birds seemed pretty enough even though
they looked as if they'd been hand-painted
by a keen but rather clumsy child.
No, what mattered was personality, character, ego.
A budgie that strutted. A budgie with swagger.

At work, at least they'd all stopped saying, "I can't believe it."
even if their eyes still told her she'd missed the last bus home
and faced a long and lonely walk in the rain.

She read the manual and prepared a cage
fit for a prince. Fresh water, a daily clean,
a mix of seeds, a cuttlefish bone,
the occasional lettuce leaf, a slice of fig.

The night Dennis announced, "I can't do this any more,"
after she'd stopped crying, she called this banquet
of his favourite foods, The Last Supper,
the condemned forced to cook their own final meal.

She placed her face the recommended distance
from his bars and repeated his name over and over,
hour after hour, day after day, until he sang in reply,
"Dennis. Dennis. Dennis. Dennis."

She knew the only fish left in the sea were those you'd throw back.
That this promising catch had slipped through her keep net.

Dennis could never resist a mirror, preening,
falling in love with himself all over again.

She taught Dennis just one more simple sentence,
one that he'd learnt remarkably quickly.

The other machinists thought it hilarious
she'd called her pet budgie Dennis.
A sign that she's getting over him,
not that there was ever much to get over.

Now when she got home, Dennis would tap
on his cage by the door, dropping a hint.

"Not long to wait, Dennis. Not long at all.
But first I need to get you a cat. For company.
I do. I do. I do. I do."
and Dennis echoed and exchanged this solemn, simple vow.

The Triumph

In the end, I only kept the one photo
of him on his bike, framed in black.
If you can have a marriage of man and machine,
this was him on his wedding night, straddled across her,
tousled hair and a self-satisfied grin on his face.

I'd watch the hours he lavished upon her.
That vigorous buffing acting as foreplay,
settling down into a rhythmic polishing and polishing
before those final, delicate strokes
when he barely seemed to be touching her at all.

Afterwards, "*I'd best take her out for a spin,
I've just been greasing her nipples.*"

Needless to say, he never greased my nipples
or any other bits come to that.
But he'd take me for a spin in the bedroom
the first Saturday night of each month,
like creosoting the fence, nothing to look forward to
yet glad to tick off once it's done.

The crash happened just where I'd expected.
He could never resist gunning her on that long, straight run
then pin-balling from road sign to lamp post to tree
before meeting the house side, head on.

"*It's like talking to a brick wall,*" he'd say to me.

The line of bikers stretched out like a black snake.
And all those wreaths shaped like motorbikes!
I swear they thought we were burying the bike not the bloke.

"*Meticulous,*" they said, spelling it out like Charades.
First syllable: mime a handshake or hug.
"*Can't believe he didn't check that.*"
I'd nod and look down like Diana.
They spared me the technical details because
I didn't know much. But I knew enough.

Now Ricky was a different kettle of fish,
drove a pimento red Triumph Herald.
When that needed a clean he'd let the rain do the job
or waited for the Scouts to come bob-a-jobbing.
Ricky put his energies elsewhere, so to speak.

All in all, I came out of my trade-in pretty well,
don't you think?

Lady Chatterley's Trial

On days like these, she wished
they'd just leave them alone,
together, their hut a country.
Their woods a continent.

But no, the prosecution was reading out an extract,
spitting out each syllable, coated with contempt.
"Not easy to know what Lawrence was driving at."
She knew exactly what he was driving at
or rather where he was driving them to:
A place where shame does not exist.

Of course, Mr Griffin-Jones lost
the moment he wondered if the jury
would let their servants read it. Servants!

If only it had been Lord Mellors
and her, simple Connie from the village,
well-endowed and eager to be taught
the joys and delights of the flesh.
Or the male ones at least.
Why then they'd be secure in some stately library
to be taken out with laboured breathing
for single-minded and single-handed pleasures.

Apparently her defence has a bishop
primed to swear on The Bible
that their sex was sacred,
a form of holy communion.
In the beginning was the word
and in the end as well
because words are what cause all the trouble.

Motorcade, 1963, Ireland

He always felt most nervous
the second an agent turned the ignition.
So many buildings. So many windows.

Switching on his trademark smile
merely hid the anxiety
in plain sight.

He was happiest when his wife
was sitting beside him.
Only a madman would risk killing
the most beautiful woman in the world.

He relaxed as he realised
the crowds seemed genuinely pleased to see him.
The waving helped, both his and theirs
as did the home-made signs.
"Thanks for coming JFK",
the letters getting smaller
like an eye-test chart,
as they ran out of room.

He made a point of looking out
for kids balanced on their pops' shoulders
like he'd done with John Junior,
novice acrobats learning the ropes.

He wondered what they'd remember
about the day The President came, if anything.
One thing was certain: he'd look back fondly
when he was safely back in the States,
in the Fall, in the Winter.

White As A Ghost

Pale White. Frail White. Ghostly White.
Sounding more like a Farrow and Ball colour chart
than an international footballer.

I once saw the magician
make himself disappear before
materialising in acres of space,
chipping the goalie, stranded in no man's land,
watching the ball bounce gently into the net
then standing, abashed,
a weekend-golfer after a hole in one.

Not handicapped by gravity,
flitting, floating, hovering over the pitch,
wearing neat ballet shoes,
not size six and a half leather football boots.

Later he signed his name for me
as if he was illuminating the Book of Kells.

Much later, in morning assembly,
as soon as the headmaster began
"Which footballer," my hand shot up,
anticipating the question like a Spurs forward
racing after a John White through ball,
"was struck by lightning, sheltering
under an oak tree on a golf course?"

Sometimes not even ghosts can move quickly enough.

Roy Woolley

Roy Woolley's recent work has appeared in *The Crank*, *Gallus* (*Poetry Scotland*), *Pulsebeat Poetry Journal*, *Consilience* and the Hammond House competition anthologies *Stardust* and *Changes*.

Signals

might begin inside a spinning wheel,
the thrum and throb of lost machinery

whose flicker pattern sets my father dreaming
about the divvy-box in the works' canteen

unsteady on a canvas chair
or how the lenses in her wartime specs

accentuate my mother's second sight
and bend the dancefloor's whitewashed lines

into a sphere whose centre lies in both of them
and makes that room an everywhere.

The twins and me are not yet ghosts
in all that glitter ball throws away,

but the rooms I'll know are waiting
and the concrete floor where I'll learn my name.

Aspects of Summer

Everything lengthens except the night and the duration of our dreams -
the stems of the rose bush, the days we're together, the whitened leaves.
Cracks in the summer house foretell some barbarous future,
but the tall glasses we fetch from the kitchen are ticking with ice.

The metal of window frames, sculptures and ornaments expands,
and the packed air is filled with crystalline songs.
Bodies locked on the lawn release heat like wine poured from a bottle,
and flies negotiate the waves from these and other fires.

Our senses are primed for the secrets a touch might reveal
over resinous tequila: I watch your hands, re-digitised with heat,
trace the flaking skin, the increased radii of the pores on my face
and the widening, corrugated weaves the sea has left on me.

The flowers stand witness, shedding their scents, open-mouthed in the sun -
the white noise of the rose, the minimalist bluebells, and the slow handclaps
of palm fronds get confused with their echoes in the compound we share.
The high red walls glitter with razor wire. There is joy in small things.

The Waiting Room

I'm a west-facing room
overlooking a garden.

Near my single sash window,
the cupboard in the corner

and an empty desk and bookcase
are lightly scuffed and scratched.

On polished boards at blood-heat,
a bluish rug deepens like a mandala.

I'm stretched across a silver lampshade
like the postcard of the painting

at mirror height above the mantelpiece.
My single window is often open,

and I hear the radio in the room below:
forecasts, threats of war, war.

Tuned Mass Damper

Ninety floors above street level, the sound waves
from the ball bouncing on a petrol-blue tile are invisible patterns
in the humid air. Molecules seethe and settle and shift again,
pushing energy outwards from chains of events dissolving in time:
my dexter hand opening; the ball accelerating earthwards;
its fluorescent material, distorting on impact and then regaining its shape;
the sphere heading back towards my palm, the dispersals of dust.
Like the hunted in Ovid, energy transforms as it seeks an escape or hides
in the stillness where a wave and its echoes interleave and cancel out.
After seven years, as this needle-bright skyscraper approaches completion,
it offers deeper perspectives on the seen and unseen elements of the city,
from the wide boulevards stretching out from the palace like burning spokes
to the fractures and dislocations the far mountains tell with white silence.
The building's foundations, sunk deep into rock and bedrock, are hidden,
unlike the golden spherical pendulum hanging four storeys below
to absorb the Earth's complex tremors and the buffeting of myriad winds
so our occupants will never feel these floors shift beneath their feet
and tremble like those hollow reeds whose rustling can resemble speech
when the ground beneath the ground they know flexes slowly in the dark.

Before the Healing Window

The Saxon angel
sings her sutra:

the rose's core,
molten from the blast

that made this roof
a roof of stars,

has cooled to glass
that, fixed in place,

resonates
with tonal blues

in curves like skaters
swirl through ice

and guides you back
to where you are.

Kitchen

I'm a key to a thousand doors, some lost forever, some of which you know. The steam is motionless behind the first door you open, and a parabola of light has settled in a copper basin.

Other doors appear, some merely shadows, some defined by noise - the clean, clear sound of china being stacked, panicked wings breaking free in a spray of blood, children repeating numbers in the dark. You're four floors up now, watching the sea when someone asks a question you still can't answer.

Some say hold what I left you; others say consider only the name, take the first letter and dive into it, dive back to the root, alter your shape so you become what you say, score this song on the glass with a diamond.

from The Hearing Woods

On a brilliant, burning day,
the grownups left for good,
insisting they deserved the time
to work out where they stood.

The twin who never left my room
looked up as I walked in.
The horizon was a heated wire
and red as butcher's string.

We watched the clouds behind us
convulse and concentrate
the streaming blues and indigoes
the streetlights would erase,

and from the velvets of his mouth,
I took the single key
that fitted all the painted doors
between the night and me.

Through rooms as empty as a thought
I'd never think again,
inverted on their polished floors,
I walked towards the stairs

and then between the scentless weeds,
around an absent car,
thinking on how vanished things
might teach you where you are.

I walked across a motorway,
a deconstructed field
where drainage from a building site
had settled like a shield

aslant against the raided ground,
like a rebus of the sky.
I knelt above that wooing dark,
gazing backwards into time.

I felt the slowing Oort cloud
find its shape through me
as synapse flooded synapse,
blurring thought and memory

and recognised the partial roads
that met and married here,
how debris from a star's collapse
might lengthen to a tear

and leave a mirror on my skin
to show me where I'd be
when I saw the path I'd made
across the undark fields.